FIRST PEOPLES

NAVAJO

VALERIE BODDEN

CREATIVE EDUCATION ✳ CREATIVE PAPERBACKS

Published by Creative Education and Creative Paperbacks
P.O. Box 227, Mankato, Minnesota 56002
Creative Education and Creative Paperbacks are imprints of
The Creative Company
www.thecreativecompany.us

Design and production by Christine Vanderbeek
Art direction by Rita Marshall
Printed in the United States of America

Photographs by Alamy (Hemis, George H.H. Huey,
INTERFOTO), Corbis (Bettmann, Corbis, Danny Lehman,
Marilyn Angel Wynn/Nativestock Pictures), Getty Images
(Bettmann, Ted Spiegel/Corbis Documentary), iStockphoto
(belfasteileen, lucky-photographer), Shutterstock (Miloje,
Tanya K, Emre Tarimcioglu)

Library of Congress Cataloging-in-Publication Data
Names: Bodden, Valerie, author.
Title: Navajo / Valerie Bodden.
Series: First Peoples.
Includes bibliographical references and index.
Summary: An introduction to the Navajo lifestyle and
history, including their forced relocation and how they keep
traditions alive today. A Navajo story recounts how two
brothers saved humanity.
Identifiers:
ISBN 978-1-60818-904-5 (hardcover)
ISBN 978-1-62832-520-1 (pbk)
ISBN 978-1-56660-956-2 (eBook)
This title has been submitted for CIP processing under
LCCN 2017940106.

CCSS: RI.1.1, 2, 3, 4, 5, 6, 7; RI.2.1, 2, 3, 4, 5, 6; RI.3.1, 2, 3, 5;
RF.1.1, 3, 4; RF.2.3, 4

First Edition HC   9 8 7 6 5 4 3 2 1
First Edition PBK   9 8 7 6 5 4 3 2 1

TABLE *of* CONTENTS

SOUTHWESTERN HOGANS

The Navajo lived in the American Southwest. They called themselves *Diné*. This meant "The People." The Spanish gave them the name Navajo.

 Steep-sided buttes are common landforms in the American Southwest.

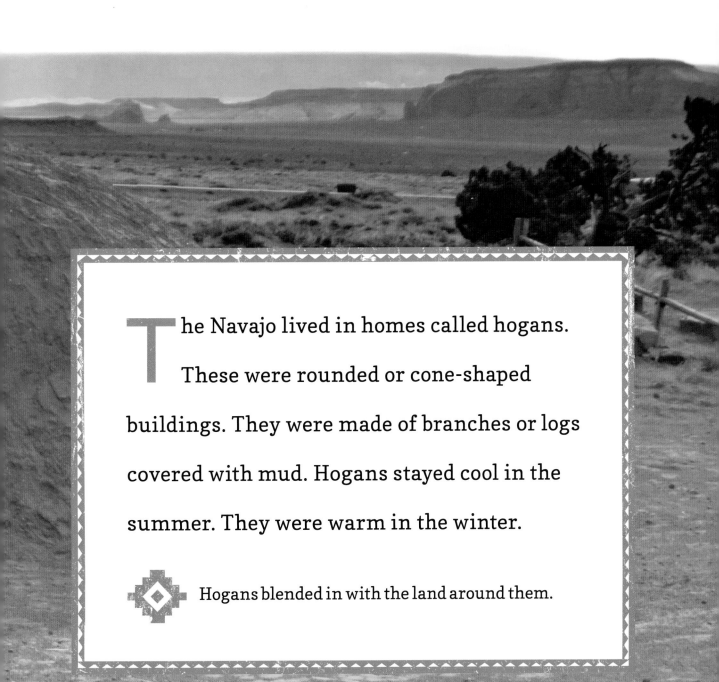

The Navajo lived in homes called hogans. These were rounded or cone-shaped buildings. They were made of branches or logs covered with mud. Hogans stayed cool in the summer. They were warm in the winter.

◆ Hogans blended in with the land around them.

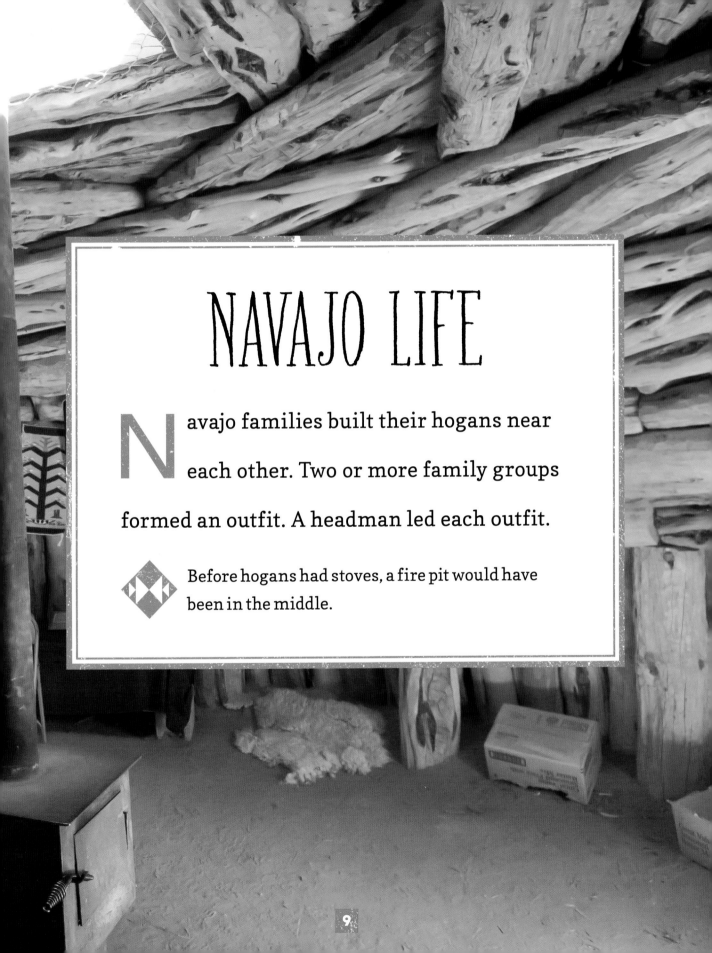

NAVAJO LIFE

Navajo families built their hogans near each other. Two or more family groups formed an outfit. A headman led each outfit.

Before hogans had stoves, a fire pit would have been in the middle.

The Navajo farmed. They grew corn, beans, and squash. They gathered acorns, sunflower seeds, and cactus fruits. They raised sheep for meat and wool. The women wove the wool into blankets.

Navajo women used what the land and animals gave them.

N avajo men hunted deer, mountain lions, and turkeys. They fought in wars. Sometimes they stole sheep and horses. Some men made silver jewelry.

Warriors like Manuelito (above) are gone, but men still make jewelry (left).

NAVAJO CEREMONIES

The Navajo believed in many GODS. They held a lot of CEREMONIES. They made sandpaintings for most ceremonies. They used sand, pollen, and flower petals for the paintings.

Sandpaintings, or drypaintings, could cover 9 to 400 square feet (0.8–37.2 sq m).

SETTLERS AND RESERVATIONS

I n the late 1500s, Spanish SETTLERS came to the Southwest. The Navajo stole their sheep. The settlers took Navajo women and children. They sold them as slaves.

 Navajo rock art shows when they came into contact with Spanish horses.

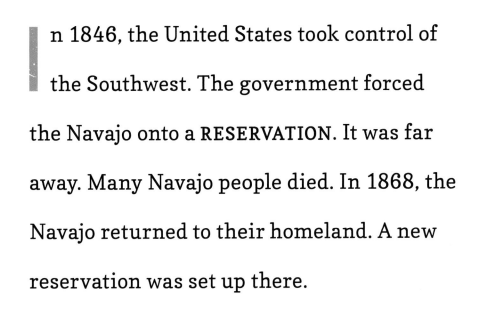

I n 1846, the United States took control of the Southwest. The government forced the Navajo onto a RESERVATION. It was far away. Many Navajo people died. In 1868, the Navajo returned to their homeland. A new reservation was set up there.

 Some reservation homes in the 1900s were not made like usual hogans.

BEING NAVAJO

Today, most Navajo still live on the reservation. Some live in hogans. Many make blankets and jewelry. They keep their TRADITIONS alive.

 Tribes like the Navajo still use eagle feathers in ceremonial clothing.

A NAVAJO STORY

The Navajo spent winter nights telling stories about the world. One story was about two gods named the Hero Twins. They wanted to save their people from monsters. They asked their father, the Sun, to help. The Sun gave them lightning. The Hero Twins used the lightning. They struck the monsters. The monsters turned into huge stones. The stones still stand over Navajo lands today.

GLOSSARY

CEREMONIES ✦ special acts carried out according to set rules

GODS ✦ beings that people believe have special powers and control the world

RESERVATION ✦ an area of land set aside for American Indians

SETTLERS ✦ people who come to live in a new area

TRADITIONS ✦ beliefs, stories, or ways of doing things that are passed down from parents to their children

READ MORE

Fullman, Joe. *Native North Americans: Dress, Eat, Write, and Play Just Like the Native Americans*. Mankato, Minn.: QEB, 2010.

Morris, Ting. *Arts and Crafts of the Native Americans*. North Mankato, Minn.: Smart Apple Media, 2007.

WEBSITES

American Southwest Virtual Museum
http://swvirtualmuseum.nau.edu/
Check out pictures of the Navajo homeland and Navajo items.

Navajo People—The Diné
http://navajopeople.org/
Learn more about the Navajo of the past and present.

Note: Every effort has been made to ensure that the websites listed above are suitable for children, that they have educational value, and that they contain no inappropriate material. However, because of the nature of the Internet, it is impossible to guarantee that these sites will remain active indefinitely or that their contents will not be altered.

INDEX